THE TEACHER WHO TOLD STORIES

POEMS & FICTION

William Pruitt

ISBN: 978-81-8253-884-9

First Edition: 2022
Rs. 200/-

Cyberwit.net
HIG 45 Kaushambi Kunj, Kalindipuram
Allahabad - 211011 (U.P.) India
http://www.cyberwit.net
Tel: +(91) 9415091004
E-mail: info@cyberwit.net

Printed at VCORE CONNECT LLP.

for Steve Lewandowski

Contents

I.

Beyond Indian Pass

The Streets Where We Lived

It is wet August again, and you are about to go
to the Bahamas. It is our first summer together,
and we hold hands at the movies. Having
little else in common, we are dazzled by this
bauble made of light called "My Fair Lady"
not knowing it will take its place on some dim shelf
in a great house we don't even know we have,
the domain of shared experience stretched by time

"All at once am I ♪
several stories high"

September Rain

The bees are losing weight, have stopped making honey
the silence between the crickets' strokes is getting wider
the toads are singing more quietly
or have laid back deeper in the grass
In September rain, my ankles ache.
I'm afraid of what this great change will ask.
I believe it is asking for my crickets' legs
that I make my songs with
& my hands that trace surfaces
& divine deep springs
and my losing them will make a beautiful sound

Wedding at Black Creek Park

the day we went to the wedding
the sky was so blue
I couldn't think of a god
whose name could make it more real

after a while, you walked away
to nurse our new baby under a tree
I stood in line for beer for both of us
brought back a plate of cheese & crackers
all the way home my mother talked
about what I was like as a baby

At Algonquin Peak

Black-capped chickadee
On the tender moss,
Dragonfly flits between trapped pools
Up here even pestering flies
Keep their distance
I have the view to myself
To the west clouds filling
The valleys   swallowing each
Peak beyond Indian Pass
Far below my family
Swims in Heart Lake

Cloud

Sticks and stones can break your bones
But words can mess up your rhythm,

Thunderstorm wakens me at night's end.
Thinnest phantom flag in foggy dawn is
All I see of Point Judith Sound.

Split shingle houses with geranium window boxes
Throng affluent shore to watch coastline disappear
Only a single outboard engine tells us ocean's there

Somewhere, someone knows a
Delphinium from a blue phlox
But not here

I have come to edge of land to hear
The call of mourning doves in a cloud which
Blake sings will one day vanish

There will be a Golden Tent
Around which children will be dancing

And I won't know which one is me

Breathing Bright Air

Snow is falling on the trees, on the house,
on telephone poles, on manhole covers,
filling potholes, falling on two white horses
standing close together on the hill sloping south
to Honeoye Lake.
I help unload a truck, boxes of nuts,
bags of flour, a wooden box of apricots from Turkey.
I stretch my arms upward to the snow
and let them fall again. I stand on the street
as the clouds darken & raise my arms upward
to the snow.
Walking home after it has stopped snowing,
the side streets have changed: not slush or hard glaze,
but a clear star-like sparkle has settled,
and the clouds are heavy, shifting, fast & bright
with the promise of snow.
This morning snow has fallen again
on this house I rent, on my neighbor's house,
on Highland park, Mt. Hope cemetery, Genesee river.
It is snowing in this poem, steadily, peacefully,
illuminating bare earth, warming shelters within.

October Song

The spider sleeps swinging in the center of her bed
the grasshopper makes his way across a shingle
a blue jay skips around listening for food
I can see the cat's eye among the bush leaves.

The thick October lawn is the cat's jungle
the sap from the new-cut grass is a last fling for the bees
the fury of summer has at last loosened
the green moth flies into the spider's fleece

Squirrels swarm & burrow
acorns fall like slow hail
the falling of one brown leaf
is more golden than the holiest grail

Decorum

In the Civic Center, people summoned for jury duty stood around or sat and waited to be called. Sometimes we read or checked our cell phones, but when we stood, it was clear there were invisible lines that we could not cross, postures we could not take, expressions we could not wear, feelings we could not feign. We were in a building where law was paramount: enforcement, interpretation, punishment. We had been relieved of our guns and our outdoor minds.

We were shown a movie of how it used to be, in the days when they tied you to a rock and you proved you were innocent by drowning. It's not that way now, they told us, if we accept our responsibility as citizens.

A teen age boy was accused of date rape. It was at a party. The judge was articulate and reasonable. We were called up one by one. Each side took its turn. Have you ever been sexually assaulted? Do you know any policemen? Do you have preconceived ideas?

We missed the ways of counting off the afternoon, the beloved lengthening of shadows, the chores that made history, the trimmings of being alive. Each time someone was called, those of us who were still sitting breathed a little sigh.

Some were excused after they respectfully acknowledged requirements they could not fulfill, or when either side respectfully requested a dismissal based on clear and cited reasons.

Sometimes the judge joined the exchanges. His urbane interjections helped to clarify and relax us in an otherwise cold and forbidding place. We even laughed occasionally. There must have been sixty of us.

When the number of people sitting in the jurors' box reached twenty-five, the judge sent them into a little room with the prosecuting attorney, the defendant's lawyer and the bailiff. It was 3:30. It would be wrong to say there was any real difference between the people who had gone into the little room and those still waiting to be questioned. Except that some of us, delivered into calculating,— they only need twelve jurors, a couple of extras,— twiddled our thumbs. Some of us still hoped to go home, and had stopped caring about the girl who was raped and the boy who was charged with rape. Some of us could no more tolerate being in this building than we could being in a cell, putting off being alive indefinitely, a living death, with no crime to atone for.

The door opened at a quarter to five and the bailiff announced, — We have completed this round of questioning and we have nine jurors for trial.

Among those of us waiting to be called, one man uttered a loud groan.

The judge turned his attention from the bailiff to our group. He was not affable. His face was red. —I will have no outbursts! he said angrily. It is a privilege to be a juror! Then his voice became a deep growl. Any more disrespect to the decorum of the court will not go unpunished.

The man had broken decorum, but the judge had shifted tone. He was not smiling. We were afraid of him. He was looking at us, all of us. We had done something very bad.

Yet we were not of the law, we did not belong to the law, and we did not understand why decorum was so important to the law. But we understood that when the bailiff said, —All rise! and we rose, that was only the beginning.

II.

The More You Know, the More You Do Not Know

He Stayed Within Himself

You are pretty banged up my friend
it doesn't take much for your pinball machine to say TILT
Some loved one's dismissive word has hexed your plunger,
sent you off to timeout without any clicking balls

But now you've freed yourself of flippers and bumpers,
you spend all your time setting up dominoes in that
twisting, diabolic pathway to your heart.
I admire your care to make sure how even at the sharp turns

they all fall true. If I knew how to tell you to stop
getting down on your hands and knees and using your precious
time and productivity to set these pieces up just so,
I surely would, but you seem to be having too much fun

The Day After I Came Back

John came to my door at 11 p.m.
the day after I came back from New York,
I'd been thinking about the old friends I'd spent time with there
wondering if we were the same people now we were back then.

John needed a ride to the bus stop,
where his sister and her son awaited him.
He was going back to Greenville Technical College
in the morning. He and his sister were caring
for their mother one block over who just
had a triple bypass. She had moved here
from South Carolina for health care. They were preparing
to sue her doctor-- I guess the one they moved away from--
as soon as they could hire a lawyer. John's other sister's
father-in-law was chief of police in a nearby town

who later would be forced to resign when charged
with rubber stamping background checks
for an officer who pressured a prisoner for sex
and for covering for a cop on cocaine who
hit a pregnant woman with his car and drove away.
The chief would say it was the town supervisor
who wanted the abuser hired without vetting, the same
sup who was found to have not murdered the woman
he had been secretly having sex with, who
had been stabbed by her unstable adult son.

But this all happened after
I took John to the bus stop,

to wait with Amanda
and her four year-old
who had just lost a tooth.

Teacher

Forty years ago, as I walked in traffic, a vision of myself
at the age I am now appeared to me from above.
Beaming down like a weathered Buddha, I'd seen it all,
I'd risen above the wars of men and women,

of men and men, small hurts missed me, the great scars
of ego and relationship had been feathered in,
saying to my sore distracted self of time long gone
in the clear sky of walking home from work
You can let go now. The music never stops.

I know now that guy wasn't really me.
Maybe it was Pallas Athena, cunningly cloaked.
As if I were a threat to her precious Achilles

Will o' the Wisp

You were told you must have goals.
So you put them on. They relieved your mind
of the unbearable weight of what to do.
They let you know you were solid, and so could ignore
impulses, like fireflies. From these goals ideas grew,
repellent for the stinging gnats of sense data,
They filled a monument room immune to time

More and more, you were your goals. Less and less
were you your life. The goals distilled what you took in.
The open bowl of your being became flat screen.
That cluster of *should*
instilled by your elders
beguiled perception.

You got your ducks lined up:
the people were the lowest common denominator.
Their quicksilver will was what the wind blew in,

You could feel it in the air— in what pure air was left—
that Biden lost. Common sense his victory wasn't real.
Of the faceless hordes who can't be loved, but only pitied,
you say to your friend, *they're not like us.*
They believe anything.

Leave It Like You Found It

You give me half a glass of orange juice,
ask, — is it half empty or half-full?
I take the glass, drink it all, put it down.
— Full, I say

Wedding at Shandaken

The further one breaks into the region of origin
the deeper that region becomes

—Oil change so soon? said my mechanic.
—I took it to the Catskills last weekend,
I said, For my niece's wedding.
Shandaken, past Big Indian.

The further towards Shandaken you go
the deeper that region becomes.

In the cold & starburst night, I drove past the turn
for Firehouse Road again and again, a bouquet
of roses & stargazers in the trunk, till out of the
dark sunken woods emerged the Full Moon Resort.

After the wedding a band played.
My wife and I danced as one.
We stamped our feet on the hardwood floor.
I had nothing to drink, but next morning,
as we raised a toast to birthdays among us,
I had a hangover and told the wrong story.

I mistook the gold ring for the carousel.
I saw a connection I didn't feel.
Not what was told, but what wasn't.

I came home to spring snow Sunday night
needy for oil
needy for salt

Thought about
digging out the driveway.

The further you descend into snowy darkness
The deeper that region becomes.

Snow was gone by morning.

Awakening on the Couch

the back door
must be open
here's the white cat

Guiniver

Seven minutes early to the Y, there were no other cars around when I saw her hobble across the lot to mine. "I won't hurt you," she said. Everything after that was borne of sad frustration.

"I just...I just need... I just need to get to the bus station...My friend, no she's not my friend, she dropped me off at Tops, I don't know why, she's my sister's friend, there's no busses from there to the bus station, could you please take me there. I've been in the hospital, I need to get home to Batavia." She actually couldn't walk forward. With every stride she twisted her right leg, not putting full weight on it, but moving with a screwing or threading motion of her torso, as if she were an open jar that had to be closed with each step.

So it was about transportation. I was early; it was Sunday. I could do that.

When she got in the car, she asked if I could possibly spare the cost of a ticket to Batavia. It was fifteen dollars and something.

She said her name was "Guiniver," putting all stress on the first syllable.

I asked her what it was like to live in Batavia. She said everybody knew each other, which wasn't bad, but that meant everybody was in your business.

I didn't ask her if she was in the hospital because of her leg; she said she came to Strong from Batavia by ambulance.

I took her to the Trailways station, just in front of the train tracks. She asked me to wait while she made sure everything was all right. She got out and went in, and I wondered if she believed I would wait for her. Her hair was cut short; her face gaunt, not unattractive, but her large gray eyes were bright with pity for her chaotic self and the knowledge of the good and evil others could do her.

"It turns out a person can't get a ticket without an ID," she said in exasperation when she came back, "And she took my ID with her—she has it."

I said, "What now?"

She was getting out her tiny flip phone. "I've got to call her. She took my stuff. Hey, where's my stuff? Where's my purse? You never do that to a person." She didn't address the party by name, but spoke as if she were continuing a conversation just now interrupted. "Okay," she said, turning to me. "It's on Joseph. Or Clinton. No, just off Joseph."

"What number?" I said.

"Just drive down this street. She said she'll be standing outside the house. Here, turn left." Now we were on Avenue A, turning right the next block at Hollenbeck. We parked and she drag-legged herself a few houses ahead, then disappeared to a side entrance. After several minutes she came back. "This isn't the one," she said. After she made another call, we turned right at Avenue D and headed east. We came to the intersection of Avenue D and Joseph, and she told me she would get out here. I parked on the curb by a church lined with cars.

She got out, started walking, then came back. "You are waiting here for me," she said. Although she formed it as a declarative sentence, she said it like she was surprised and needed to clarify. When I said I was, she said to stay right there.

She disappeared around the corner. Then she came back and said, "It's in her car up ahead. I'll be right back." This time she was away longer, ten or twelve minutes. I was formulating a plan to get rid of her. I couldn't believe anything positive would come out of these phone calls. She came back exhausted and doleful. "Nothing's in there. She lied to me."

"What can you do?"

"Take me back to the bus depot. I'll text my mom. No, take me to the Y. I can wait there." It was beginning to rain. She was breathing heavily. "I've been in the hospital for a week. I'm not used to all this walking."

We were on Joseph, heading back to the bus station. "How about if you give me back the twenty and I'll buy the ticket for you."

"But that ticket would have your name on it, and the passenger wouldn't be that person."

She was texting. "Do you know where Emerson Street is?"

"Kind of." I had a vague idea it was on the west side.

"If you could take me there, I could wait till my mom gets off work."

"Why don't I take you to the bus station or the Y to wait?"

"Please, they don't want me there. This is a place where I can wait in someone's living room until my mom can come get me."

"I can't drive that far. I have things I need to do. I could drive you to the Y"— we had turned around at the bus station and were headed down St. Paul now— "and you could wait there until help comes."

"I'm not trying to be difficult," she said tearfully, "I just want to get to this place and wait there. Could you please, please take me to that place? Or take me back to the Y and I'll walk from there."

It was now raining steadily. What I didn't want was to take her to another dead-end destination. I had no reason to disbelieve her, but I had never seen her interacting with anyone, not even at the bus station. Everything about her was about *her.*

"What's the address?"

"239 Emerson." At last she told me a number. It was coming from her mother, rather than the malefactor who kept sending us in circles. I put it into my phone, and the voice from Google maps brought into the car a definiteness and precision to our quest. We turned left at Driving Park Bridge.

"Why do you text your mom instead of just calling her?"

"She's working now," she said. "If I called her it would put her at risk of losing her job. Do you have grown children?" she asked. I sensed she wanted to restore the equability between us which had been stretching thin in her need.

"Yes."

"Grandchildren?"

"Two. Eight and four."

"Four! What a great age!"

"Do you have children?"

"Yes. I have a son." She said it with the pride of accomplishment and identity. "Eleven."

When she told me he was born "just before nine eleven," I asked how could that be, he would be sixteen. She replied punctiliously, as if I were trying to trip her up, "No, I mean nine eleven, the month and day."

When we got to the address, she showed no uncertainty or doubt, as glad to turn me loose as I was to leave. "Good luck getting home," I said. She got out of the car, crossing the street to the place where she was supposed to be.

III.

Make It So

The Teacher Who Had Nothing

They are about to become women and men. They have gotten themselves to a place where if they're lucky, they might be left alone or actively engaged. People might stop doing things to them, or looking past them.

A few appreciate this opportunity. They are alert to the teacher's voice, and are just beginning to hear the spaces between his words. It is a relief to have it all in front of them.

Others are in a sea of swim. They don't know they are not in that sea now. They don't hear the silence within the teacher's sentences, or the sentences. They don't see the imminent adult the teacher sees as he looks at them. They are still being pinched, probed, touched, threatened. cajoled, excoriated, praised, fussed over, or systematically ignored. Even on this island of replenishment, they are beset by aromatic umbilical memories so strong the teacher can smell the onions and green peppers in the deep fry of their attention, or less noticeable, the slowly whitening mold of neglect.

He is teaching them the language of the place their lives have brought them to. They don't yet know the size or applications of the subject. He starts by asking them to interview each other. He pairs up strangers, or the least familiar of acquaintances. He hopes nobody falls in love too hard. He has great compassion and nothing to impart or instill.

He wants them
        to at least
get a taste,
                to be free, for a moment,
of each other,

of him.
Of themselves.

He wants them to see
there is something more for language than communication.

Missed Classes Dream

Bringing in the sheaves
Bringing in the sheaves
We will come rejoicing
Bringing in the sheaves
American Gospel Hymn

I'm taking courses at a summer institute on a bright, shiny campus.
I've missed classes, wonder what kind of grade I'll pull.
Maybe I'll get by with just being myself,
The ones who count can see I'm a good student.

We go with our professor
into a gleaming building of blinds and glass.
I hear someone say —It's all ruined. Someone has broken in
and destroyed lab equipment. Burners are scorched.
Digital scales, smashed. I notice how quiet my teacher is.
There is no anger at the fundamentalists, just
sorrow and disbelief. *Why would someone do this*, his eyes say.

Even though I think I know the answer,
I feel different being around someone like him.
I resolve to work harder, do what's needed.

Correcting Myself in a Dream

Walking in the city, I see food displayed in a restaurant window.
I feel sorry that no one will come because of Covid.
I buy one or two funny-looking croissants with bumpy pink
frosting.

I walk slowly with friends when one of them
reminds me we have to be somewhere.
—Will you stop? I say. I wish we were
somewhere in the thirteenth century
when people weren't always rushing around.
Of course that *was* the century of Bubonic Plague.

She says, —Is that when the plague was?
I say after considering, —Actually, the 14th,

Do It Now

I dream I'm on a long walk home
I leave the soda shop with the glass
    I was drinking from
I'll return it later I think but when
I have to stop for something else
I decide, instead of putting it off
to return it now

Now I'm walking home from school with a girl
It all seems like a dream she says and
I wonder if she knows how right she is

We're in a small corridor when she mentions
she is looking for something for her boyfriend
I recognize this might be my only chance
I kiss her—I want you to know I love you.
Her casual manner changes. —What?
I say it again and she looks
at me as if the world has changed
through some small thing

I was applying the lesson of my dream in my dream
one step removed from the way that woman
did it whom the Haudenosaunee tell of
who simply woke up and told her husband
to change the world the way she dreamed it and he did:
that dream, that legend that became this waking world
the same one I'm trying to wake up from now

Six Dreams

1.

Performing for adults, the storyteller is tentative.When he says, —he liked doing things for others because it felt like it was for himself, a woman snorts, —I bet. He thinks, *of course. She's a journalist.* But in his heart he knows he has failed as a storyteller.

2.

I think of using a different tone when I speak, how by changing my emphasis at the end of a sentence, I would sound more assertive, less naive. I wonder if I have the guts to do it. Something about the thought of it frightens me, as if I wouldn't be able to carry it off and still understand what I'm saying.

3.

A doctor tells a man
he needs the healing therapy
of grass and mud.
The man asks his wife
if she knows where there's an old towel.

4.

—Ok. tell me who I'm taking to the party.

She leaned across the table and placed her fingers on the lens of his glasses. He couldn't see anything. She leaned back, leaving him in darkness.

—Petersen, she said, looking at him.

5.

A man's wife asks him to retrieve some pans and cookie tins. In a little valley with pink and red skies, he goes to a new plaza of brightly lit, pastel-colored shops in the town where he used to work, He sees an old rusty shopping cart in one store with what must be his stuff in it. He says to the proprietor, — This is strange, but I think these are my tins. So I'll just take them. You probably don't want this cart in your new store, so I'll take it too.

The owner says, —I was wondering about that cart.

Leaving the store, the man thinks he will abandon the cart somewhere before he gets home.

6.

I am Odysseus
hiding in the room
where I grew up

waiting for my friends
so we can hatch out a plan
to make our escape
from Polyphemus.

He knows what we're doing
He's delighted by the game.
He has no notion of us winning.
I have no doubt we'll take him down.

He only has one eye
and we see
what we surround.
His name means
"abounding in songs and legends"

School Mode

After all these years, to be
Still stuck in School Mode
But it's not
Next
It's
This

To My Daughter on the Occasion of Her High School Graduation

Last night there was thunder & rain,
ramifying branches of lightning,
like the night before you were born,
when power went out & we joked
a big event must be about to happen

Today your graduation arrives with
wood thrush music in the morning after the storm
but I didn't know that black bird in the back yard
with the flat call, and wings with a touch of white

Stephen Jay Gould tirelessly reminds us
evolution is not progress, adaptation
is not better than before, but
addressing the new circumstances
(Different from a moment before!)

Primitive is not dumber or slower
more complex not higher
newer not necessarily improved.
Evolution, you, branch
out like a tree, higher, but
the main growth is outward.
Growth is good.
Maybe you can see the horizon now.

Like lightning, in an instant you have come this far.
But time is all one lightning flash.
The trunk is still there, the heartwood
I held in my arms the night
that you first saw the light

The Teacher Who Told Stories

They were about a dozen teenagers newly arrived in America, they were from Honduras, Ukraine, Mexico, Moldova, Vietnam, Poland. As he stood before them, feeling the way they moved at their tables (they sat at tables rather than desks), the way their eyes moved, how they held their heads, he noticed something unusual. The students were nearly all at the same level of understanding English: mostly they didn't.

There was usually a wide range of English fluency among any group of students from other countries, even when they were all classed "beginners." But these kids, he saw, were *beginners*.

If you were observing this group and had never seen an ESL class, you might have thought they were learning-impaired; everything moving so slowly, the teacher constantly repeating, using his body, his hands to express, writing words on the board to illustrate what he was saying; so shadowy and tentative was everything, broken up only by the teacher's modulation in tone, his funny self-dramatization and storytelling impulses --for that is what he was, a storyteller--constantly sending out little life jackets and inner tubes to rescue them from drowning in language.

At one time in his life, his only goal had been to achieve enlightenment, which he had conceived in terms of stillness and silence and solitude. When that didn't work-- things kept moving and making sounds whether he wanted them to or not-- he made a compensating discovery: he could be among people if he had something to do. If he couldn't force them to just stop and stay where they were forever and save them from death, at least he could divert them. But he had to keep his eye on them.

Often it was difficult if they mostly spoke the same language and used that language with each other to understand. But this class couldn't do that so much; their origins were too disparate, except for two pairs of siblings, a Ukrainian sister and brother, and two Moldovan sisters, all of whom spoke Ukrainian.

There was something else about this class. They were smart. Especially in the girls' cases, (the class was mostly girls), the relaxed way they looked at him while they listened, the way they turned their pages and wrote in their journals in their native language, he could tell they had enough self-esteem to understand that this was a job, a task they had to accomplish, not a punishment for some failure of their own; and that they had enough intelligent energy to keep listening when almost everything they heard was noise.

Most of them, that is. The brother-and-sister siblings were Alexander and Sofia, and Alexander, at fifteen mostly elbows and legs, was affixed to the idea that he had to understand everything to understand anything. As the teacher spoke and watched, he could feel the boy getting a headache. Finally Alexander buried his face in his hands, and when he looked up, his expression showed dull stupefaction, even when the teacher knew he was giving him everything he needed to understand.

Amalia, the older of the other pair of siblings was the opposite. Amalia was slim, with light smooth skin, dark hair and vivacious eyes, and a background expression of thoughtful presence. It didn't take long from her responses before the teacher understood she was using the very few words or phrases she could comprehend to link to new words, all the while disregarding what she didn't understand, thus rapidly extending her grasp of English so that, after just a few weeks, she was having meaningful, if slow, conversations with the teacher, and with others.

He noticed how singular was her visible cerebration, her elegant, self-effacing composure in the face of uncertainty; how this effect rippled outward: to Amalia's sister, Crina, light-haired and genial, quicker to speak than Amalia, but smiling and frowning at the same time, as if she could not believe the strange sounds coming out of her mouth; to Sofia,

Alexander's sister, seventeen, but with a receptive playfulness in her eyes that told the teacher exactly how she must have looked ten years before; to Nguyet, Vietnamese, quieter and more of a beginner than the others, if that was possible, whose shades of feeling would mystify him as they crossed her face; to Maribel, from Honduras, who sat in the back, with oval face, large eyes and knowing smile, beautiful, unflappable, wise and kind; to Eberto, from Mexico, tall and comically excitable, who would turn his head and squint his eyes as if what he wanted to say was too bright to look at directly; to Pascuala, from a migrant family from Mexico; and the rest.

Alexander and Sofia and Crina and Amalia all belonged to the Slavic Pentecostal Church, a large and growing congregation in a new building. The teacher was impressed by how quickly the girls learned to communicate with each other in English and how easily they took in Maribel, the outsider, the non-Pentecost.

—Let's take a walk, he said on the first day, going outside as they learned not only the English names of the cardinal directions, but where they were here in this new place they had come to, and this would be a precursor to the Social Studies curriculum he was also certified to teach.

—Let's have interviews, the teacher said on the fourth day of class, when they were all there for the first time. He paired Amalia with Pascuala and Crina with Nguyet and Alexander with Maribel and Eberto with Sofia. What would you like to know about your classmates? He wrote questions on the board. Date of birth place of birth how many siblings birth-order. When where how? What's the last movie you saw What kind of music do you like Why did you come here? He called in Vickie, a secretary from the office to model interviewing. When Vickie asked him how many brothers and sisters he had, and he replied "none," it was the first time the entire class looked at him with utter incomprehension.

It was the day they did interviews that planes struck the Towers and the Pentagon.

As the year went on, he noticed how this class to a great extent could teach itself, which meant that he had to rely less than ever on discipline, which was exactly as he liked. He preferred to treat his students with informal respect, affection and gruff but purposeful humor. It didn't always work. Teenagers mostly got his gentle needling and deadpan sarcasm, but once when Crina expressed an opinion and he said —Nobody cares, intending a joke, what he got were Crina's tears. —Why would you say such a thing? she broke down, and he understood he had stepped on a sore place which hurt more than it could be explained away.

As months went by, he taught them poetry, so they could experience when sound and meaning did converge, smoothing the path to understanding: "I Hear America Singing." The *Songs of Experience*. "Little fly thy summer's play/My thoughtless hand has brushed away." He gave them proverbs, aphorisms and idioms to enlarge their working vocabulary and to introduce them to metaphor. When they read the fable "The Fox and the Grapes," they learned there was an idiom, *sour grapes*. Once when Alexander came back from a test he had been studying especially hard for, and the teacher asked him how he did, he said, —I failed. But I don't care. Immediately the teacher pointed at him, and said, —Sour grapes! and Alexander smiled.

One winter morning he asked them if they believed in evolution, and why or why not. Maribel said she did because it was a fact of science. Alexander and Sofia were shaking their heads.Crina said,—I…don't think… people come from monkeys…God make humans.

The teacher said, —Well, evolution says people and monkeys are like cousins, come from an ANCESTOR, writing the word on the board. —But does that make God… gone? Can there be evolution and God? What do you think, Amalia?

Everyone looked at her. She looked to the floor, between the seats, up at the ceiling, pondering without straining, turning her head at different angles, craning her neck as if she were trying to see if something was there or not. —I don't think…ummm…evolution means…no God.

It may have been in that exchange the teacher developed a crush on Amalia. There was something impeccable about her, something casually immaculate. He didn't have to worry about behaving inappropriately with her. He didn't long for her. She appeared to him as an ikon, a swinging pendulum, engaged but unattached, and in her engagement was compassion, curiosity, intelligence, pity, perhaps love. As she listened and thought, her expression made him think she was waiting for the silence after the last sound uttered, for the door to close, the meaning to click, for the whole story of the sentence to be told. He took comfort in looking at her as from afar: in another life, she would be a queen, and he would be her knowing and devoted servant.

He taught them about haiku. Once he read a poem by Issa to them:

> Cold rain on the roof. I think
>
> of my childhood: was it only a dream?
>
> Was I really young once?

He looked up. They were all looking at him. Nobody said a word. Finally Eberto said, —Oh, teacher. You shouldn't read us that one.

What happened to this class? People scattered, as they will. Nguyet went to graduate school. Alexander and Sofia's family moved to North Carolina. Eberto went back to Mexico, and taught Technical English. Maribel had a baby. Then she had another. Pascuala went to Florida and came back in the spring. Crina got married and became very agitated with the teacher when he could not come to her wedding, even though he explained that he had taken on a summer job out of town, and could not get back. He heard that Amalia was sick and missed a lot of school; he thought of her with concern. He knew she did not get married, and guessed it was related to health issues, as Pentecostal girls always got married.

The Slavic Pentecostal Church kept growing, and this led to more students for the teacher, and a more complicated life. For as his classes grew larger, and more predominantly Ukrainian, he had to alter his way of teaching. For one thing, he could not as easily teach them English by appealing to their curiosity about the world, since their church had taught them about it already. This seemed to affect their ability to associate. It was as if he would point to the moon, and they could only look at his finger instead of the moon.

The Slavic Pentecostals were peacefully invading the U.S. in the same wave of fundamentalism with which terrorists were trying to grip the world, the same wave that evangelicals in America rode to prominence reinforcing Biblically inspired belief; everywhere, truth was becoming more dependent on the Word.

Even education became more literal. Research indicated that what students most needed was to learn to think, to reflect, to examine their values and explore meaning, but schools in fact did just the opposite: as they became more centralized, they framed the absolute factuality of the curriculum. Testing became ubiquitous, the only true form of assessment. The most important feature of the student to the school was the test score, and of the teacher to the school was the evaluation score, which was dependent on the test score. Teaching the Socratic method, modeling values and exploring meaning were left to families and the church, along with field trips and movies. The most valued quality became that which could be measured.

Through it all, the teacher continued his way, telling stories whenever the opportunity arose: at Halloween, when fundamentalist churches insisted schools couldn't celebrate it, but some did anyway; at seasonal assemblies, though these diminished as testing took over the organization of the school schedule; and especially in his own Social Studies class, which he taught as a series of stories, such as the sinking of the Lusitania. —There is always more than one cause for anything, he said in class, but still it was true that the captain of the Lusitania had been warned that the ship would probably be a target for torpedoes, and that he should run a zig-zag pattern to avoid them. He drew the pattern on the board, and told his students how the captain wouldn't do that because he thought it might make the passengers *fearful*; eleven hundred ninety-eight people died.

He told them how in Germany the Hawks of 1914 who wanted war and held power almost until the end, handed it to the moderates *only when they saw they were going to lose;* and how these moderates were the ones forced to sign the humiliating Treaty of Versailles, and were consequently blamed, along with the Jews, for giving Germany away. He wanted them to know that history was comprehensible, even as fundamentalists championed facts only, which removed all meaning. Then the state got rid of the controversy by demonstrating that history wasn't about anything except history.

Sometimes he enjoyed the notion that he was just apparently an ESL teacher, but secretly and subversively teaching "values," which he couldn't do so blatantly if he were not teaching English as a Second Language. But he did love the elements of language: the vocabulary and grammar and syntax that created meaning. Like the fairy godmother, he knew they had to see the whole process: the impulse, the pain, the loss; the garden, the mice, the pumpkin. The grammar! But he was careful not to stop before the story was told, complete: and it had to end by midnight. How many stories had he told, how many mice passed under the eye of the sleeping cat, how many midnights flashed in a whirl!

In the spring of his last year of teaching, with only a month to go, he noticed on the morning attendance email, a familiar name among the list of substitutes: teaching home ec (a.m. only): Amalia Buc'ã! He caught her in the lobby on her way out, suggested they drive their cars to a coffee shop down the street.

As he drove to meet her, he reveled in his good fortune. To find an old student at this time, at the end of his teaching career. And that it should be Amalia! And that there should be time and place for them to sit down and talk. As she sat opposite him in the coffee shop, (she had declined food, saying she didn't eat lunch, so he ordered tea for her and coffee for him), he was amazed to hear her chatter to him, just as women do, in the rush of catching up, a kind of breathy confiding, as if skipping over things because there was so much to say. It was a treat to be confided in with such apparent frankness, to hear *her* being chatty, even ordinary, so rarefied a niche he had positioned her in. She was speaking of having fibromyalgia, of having to miss a lot of school, of having gotten her degree in education, of just now finding work.

He noticed her skin was coarser; she had a scar below her right cheekbone, and he wondered if that was possibly related to fever. She was slightly heavier, and she moved stiffly, so the weight gave the appearance of constraining her. She seemed to have a slight limp. Her eyes had dulled, though she smiled at him. She assured him that she was all right now. —I was worn out. I had to stop everything. Now I tell everyone, my mom, my dad, *we mustn't work so hard.* It surprised him a little when she said that, and the way she said it, with such dramatic emphasis. When she repeated it a few sentences later, there was a slow, vertiginous dawning.

After he had told her briefly about his teaching career winding down, she said, —Do you believe in God? and he caught the faintest hint that this was a question on which the rest of their relationship would depend.

—Yes, he said, But I don't like it when people talk about him, or claim to know what he thinks. This was true, but he still felt guilty for asserting and qualifying it under pressure. She nodded to show understanding, and continued to talk about how important it was that people experience God through themselves, and not through what other people say, or worse, pretend.

But he wasn't attending too closely to what she was saying, partly because he could tell that it was intended for a more general audience than for him directly; but he also caught something in her way of speaking. Although she still had her Slavic tones and sibilance, she had improved as an English speaker enough for him to recognize that she had eased into a role beyond language, a role he had never imagined her playing.

He heard the voice of prudent constraint, the unmarried aunt, not just an older sister. She had passed him in the act of aging. He saw that the sickness that had set her apart from her community and made her different to them, now made her different in her own eyes too.

When the voices of children are heard on the green,

And whisperings are in the dale,

The days of my youth rise fresh in my mind,

My face turns green and pale.

She was no longer the girl whose bright thought scanned the darkness of her mind for what things meant, for how she felt. There was a shadow now, a check, that had turned this sitting down together, this rich exchange, into a role play in an echo chamber: *everything will be okay if we don't work so hard* was her answer to every question. In the moment between contingency and learned response, the whole world had disappeared.

They exchanged various numbers. He remained the Teacher, encouraged her to use him as a reference for jobs. He left with the feeling he had absorbed an invisible blow.

He went home, looked out his window, and saw the world had opened. It was full spring, and it was the day of garbage pick up. Most of the magnolia blossoms had fallen on yellow crates with empty wine bottles and pickle jars askew, and a cardboard tube sticking out. Across the street, maple trees showed a breeze in the most subtle flickering of leaves which were not there last week.

IV.

It's Like This

No Secrets

I used to think everything was hidden;
Girls naked in dorm rooms and shower stalls,
Lovers lying in houses with one light on late.
I felt deprived and pierced by women I didn't know

How hard to go behind the facade of the face,
To hear speech's double meaning of sound and intent,
To cross the light years to someone's portico.

An angel kissed me, no other way to say it,
I'm sorry she hasn't kissed you, or maybe she has,

In which case you know this is it.

Beyond Our Noise

The paterfamilias to his inamorata, post-coitus:

—I mean what I say, know what I mean?
Which includes what I don't say.
I am what I do, and that
Includes what I don't do,
Meaning is part of what is.

—Have you noticed the quiet around us
When we have sex these days, my Dear?
It's probably because those Bardo beings
don't gather around like they used to.

(In some forms of Buddhism, all who die enter the Bardo, a formless realm where they must wait to be reincarnated into karmic life.)

If You Break It It's Yours

Focus your mind like a dog on a bone, said our teacher
One of us asked. is the goal to be like a dog?
Teacher smiled, no. Not to be like a dog.
When Teacher said, if you look closely,

You won't find an I, some of us got scared.
We loved I. "Like a drunkard his wine."♪
Till I betrayed us by turning out to be in it for itself.
Now caught between I and not-I, we began to attend

To what was around us which was when
We noticed the mirror was not like the rest of the furniture,
Teacher said it was no big deal if it had a little dust.
What we see in its reflection though, should be clear.

By the way, she said. If you break it it's yours. Always was.

Pelonis Table Fan

The atoms inside the guard on the Pelonis table fan
brim with energy. The guard doesn't move,
but the scores of thin white spokes tightly spaced around
the motor housing in radiating grooves
contain arcane migration.
Those atoms jitter, drift, vibrate,
even if it's absolute zero in the room.
A brace of hoops binds the spokes
which expand outward to the rim.

The guard moves in stillness,
it carries the old secret, the same hidden
movement we can't see of mountains and boulders
and stones, this guard that protects

the blades of the Pelonis
table fan from me, and me from the blades,
every morning in formation, every second firm,
moving inside itself, power manifest as rest
as the Tao Te Ching might say.

Creation Studio

Jacques Vallée says where we used to see angels
is now Area 51

Where we used to see God, now it's said
we're in a simulation

But any artist can see we're characters still developing
In a story whose plot is being worked out as we speak

To do Art is more
than to engineer.
Forget Intelligent Design,
how about
Sentient Intention

Life, thought, characters. evolve.
We start as a single cell.
How can we not sometimes feel small?
Along the way, we pick up a little free will.
All the time doing what we can.
She's pleased when we surprise her, even if it's nasty.

Red Maples near the Hudson

have roots of slanting fractured rock you think,
at the site of the shale outcropping
just west of the walking bridge in Poughkeepsie

Diaspora

Although we are over four hundred miles from the sea
The legions of trees on the street at sunrise on Saturday
This last day of summer are pelagic,
Restless with tidal movement
As if they were all getting their things together
Before starting the long trip down from the last high peak
To places where we can't see or find each other

A squirrel sits in shadow just below
Sunlight slowly pouring into the yard
A coffee-colored dogwood leaf falls into my coffee
Blackbird pursues a shrieking crow
Old cat chases a squirrel up the magnolia
Now Crow stands in the middle of the street

No cars today, just the trees tossing, talking,
We're taking a deep breath now,
Fix this moment in your memory,
Our breath in this light will feed you
In days to come,
And the sun says,
See it's like this, little leaves of bejewelled
Mountain ash fly up, up, as Crow sits
In the topmost dead branch of the old bent-over birch

Don't Let Go

"Harm and suffering have no objective existence; what gives them their existence and their power is only our aversion to them."

Sogyal Rinpoche, *The Tibetan Book of Living and Dying*

♪ "Hear that whistle, it's ten o'clock"

Roy Hamilton, *Don't Let Go*

The question is not *Is it a dream or is it real.* We know it is real because we are denied the pure poetry of him simply leaving. He will stay until every legal avenue is exhausted, until every one of us who lives by law feels exhausted.

We also know it's real because of arthritis, Covid, unemployment checks in the mail, or not in the mail. Because of slights from loved ones and the cold wind off the lake.

But being real doesn't make it not a dream.

No, the question is, *Is it a dream or is it not a dream?* Because if it's not a dream, what is it?

I say, *I am existing. This is my life. This is this.* As long as I say that, this *is* this.

But when I let go of this life, when I let myself be lost in that mundane realia we have filled it with to pretend it is not a dream, when this is not *this,* then I no longer behold it, then it becomes something that is not real, not dream, not *this.*

Freedom of will. To behold your life, or not.

December 2020

Dream Time in Bubble Land

Saturday

(A sixty five year-old man died yesterday when his car crossed the center line and hit a Mack truck about ten miles north of Stowe...)

—Once there was an old man who had a pet rooster with a golden comb.

And he also had a clever little cat with green eyes.

One day the old man said, Puss my dear, I have to go out and knock down some trees to pay the rent. I want you to bring me a nice hot lunch at noon. And little Peter Cock can stay and mind the house.

Huh! thought the rooster. Why can't I go too? Master doesn't trust me. Nobody trusts me. Boo-hoo-hoo-hoo!

The girl could see the rooster standing on the back of a chair, probably an overstuffed chair like the one her dad sat in when he came home from work, one with plenty of room to move around on the back.

Now the rooster was crying. Everyone was laughing. The girl looked up at her mother who was smiling, and moved closer.

A portal was formed, multiplied by the dozens who sat on the grass or stood or leaned against trees, some watching themselves as they listened, others quickly unfolding the strands the teller provided and passing through. It was these last who slipped out of time that late September afternoon.

****

Doreen Brennan looked at the fish on the cutting board. *How hard could it be*? She brought her laptop into the kitchen and set it on the counter. She pulled up a You Tube video and hit play. Her phone announced her sister's ring tone. She put the video on pause.

—Hi, Erin.

—What are you doing?

—Cleaning a fish.

—You went fishing?

—No, a client brought it. I'm gonna cook it for us tomorrow night.

—Oh.

—It's just dinner.

—Anybody I know?

—Henry, you know him I think. He goes to that church at St. Paul and East Ridge.

—Well I got another catch of the day for you.

—Talk to me.

—This is what happens when you're untethered. Remember Robert Haney?

—Should I?

—Last month at Harper's arts night. I introduced you to him.

—Oh, the superintendent.

—Yeah. He asked me yesterday if you were with anybody, I said no and he asked for your number.

—Hmm. I guess it's okay. So he's not married?

—I always figured him for gay. Guess not.

—Or I'm a closet accessory. I gotta go. I've got this fish with a head that needs to come off.

****

Milly Roark pulled her jeans up over her hips, her firm breasts jiggling with the effort. —I think I heard you read the news once.

—Couldn't have, said Jim Fowler. My station didn't transmit this far.

—When I went to Syracuse. How long were you on the radio?

—Just two years.

—I liked that story you told today, she said, zipping up. Where'd it come from?

—From a book. Where I get most of 'em.

—I didn't know you played guitar. All the kids liked it. Adults too. *Peter Cock*. She gave him a sly smile. Her large eyes, oval face and clear skin exuded an air of health and expressiveness.

—I forgot, said Jim, Did you tell me you grew up on a farm?

—That must be your girlfriend in the next town. My dad is a grade school teacher and my mom's a professor.

—Right, he said. He was checking his pants pockets. He was looking for the check he got for the performance. It was hard to keep track of things, especially when he took off his pants in the middle of the day. He found it, he thought, but no, it was the note Milly had given him. *Meet me in your room after*, with a smiley face. Looking at it had given his performance an extra oomph.

—I actually don't have a girlfriend in the next town, he said slowly, moving through multiple pockets of his fishing jacket. There it is. She looked at him doubtfully. Why didn't you bring your kids? he asked.

—They're spending the day with Jerry. She sat down next to him on the bed and he put his arm around her shoulder. She took out a brush and began working it through her long, luxuriant hair. He just got back from a two month business trip. They're just two and four. They're too young for a storytelling.

—No they're not. At least, the four year-old isn't. The little one could sit in your lap.

—But I brought some news that's just for your ears.

—What news would that be?

Her voice went low. She stopped brushing, her eyes full of knowledge, —It's about something you gave me.

He waited a beat. The tone of her voice told him.

—Really? he said. Another beat. Just that once?

She nodded gravely.

He took a deep breath and took his arm away. —Jesus. I thought you were taking the pill.

—I was. She got up and put the brush back in her bag, the diamond on her finger catching a glint from the late afternoon sun. Don't worry about it. It's good timing. I'll tell him it's his. You don't look that different from each other. At least up above. What's the matter?

—Nothing, he said. Glad to hear this is so easily resolved.

She looked at him quizzically, got up and walked over to pick up the rest of her clothes. —You think you should be with Doreen.

—No. It's like betting your life savings on the Super Bowl. Win or lose, it's no fun watching.

—You're not just watching, she whispered huskily. Then she threw on a loose pullover. But I've got you covered, she said.

—I told you Doreen and I are done.

—Remember the story you told last time? she said, fixing her collar. Red Robe's Dream? If the searcher can find even the tiniest bone splinter among the ashes, it's not done. Tell me she didn't cross your mind just now.

—I thought I had a career. A friend gave me a tab of acid and everything changed. Couldn't go through the motions anymore. Couldn't stand hearing myself. I'd be reading about a fatal hit and run and have to remember not to sound like a waiter reciting specials of the day. And who cares about the freaking weather? It's all just hocus pocus.

—I thought they were getting more accurate.

—I'm not talking about technology. A few need to know. House painters, construction supervisors, airport traffic control. Umpire crews. For the rest of us it's pretending to have control. An obsession to know *what's coming*. A bad habit. It's not alcohol or gambling that the national addiction, it's the need to predict.

—So you quit and became a storyteller. Guess Doreen wasn't too pleased.

—No, she wasn't. But we were sharing expenses, and she was willing to give it a shot. I took a class in storytelling, I met this woman in the folk tale section of a bookstore, Hannah. She was a storyteller too. We went to a workshop on the coast. We talked the whole way. We had a lot to say to each other.

—Did you fall in love with her?

—I was smitten, not besotted. We did an exercise at the workshop where you look into each other's eyes for three minutes without speaking, and then say what you learned about your partner.

—But that's cheating if you did it with Hannah. You already knew about her.

—No, I learned about what she couldn't tell me in words. On afternoon break, we put out in a canoe on Crescent Lake and tipped over. I came with home with pneumonia.

—What did Doreen say?

—After I recovered? She kicked me out. I shouldn't have left without a fight. It was because I was still weak. That and the fact that it was her house.

—So go back to her.

—Hmm. She'll have a bunch of bumble bees buzzing around her flowers.

Milly came over, took him by his shirt, pulled his face close to hers. —That thing I told you just now might be true, Or it might be I wanted to get your attention. It might be I wanted to see what you looked like when you weren't pretending. Either way, you've got an insight. She kissed him hard on the lips and walked out of the room.

Sunday

(There will be freezing rain tonight with a low in the upper 20s but we can look forward to clearing skies tomorrow. Complete forecast, after...)

Doreen awoke and let the day come to her as she lay in bed. If Jim were here, they would probably be having sex. There was approaching color in the dawn sky. She put on some clothes and walked into the back yard at the edge of the suburban woods. No one else was out. She sat down on the grass and leaned against her house. Paper birches were just now showing their turn to yellow in the growing glow behind them.

She thought of her niece in high school, how they were always telling you, *Be a leader. Follow your dream. Have goals.* They just forgot to say, *but not everybody. And not quite yet, only after we've finished filling your head with what we want you to think.* Nobody seemed to care about the gap between goals and actual dreams, which made it unlikely anybody would understand what dreams were. And they didn't want you to notice the big invisible hand the goals had to be chosen from.

She was glad those times were gone. Was she glad Jim was gone? She wasn't sure. She did miss getting laid.

****

Henry Longar sat in his porch rocking chair eating a bowl of Wheaties with slices of banana before church and pondered once again, why wasn't he married? Every other man his age in church was.

He did not notice the clay pot of succulents at this feet, but gazed preoccupied at the cosmos lining both sides of the crumbling front walk. The suspicion continued to grow that if he limited the field to his church, he would come up empty. He had hesitated and the options had quickly shrunk. Now the eligible ones were getting to be a little young, even if you included the congregation across town. He had not been thinking big enough. He lacked confidence in his ability to proselytize. Fortunately, an angel had saved him.

He slipped completely into reverie. The mystery of God's moves revealed in the church picnic. How he had bent at the waist to catch a softball and his legs collapsed and he couldn't get up; how his friends gathered around him and decided his back wasn't broken and carried him home instead of to the hospital, where he probably would have taken longer to heal and never met her; how she came to his house because somebody—was it Marybeth Blankenship?— had her number. She wasn't even a chiropractor, but she knew kinesiology and what had happened to him. *Extruded disc*, she called it. She barely touched him— he carried the memory of her fingertips on his skin— and told him to stay on his back for three weeks. She came twice more and touched him the same way. He did what she said and got up, pain-free. A miracle.

He still went to her although he didn't need to, but she didn't know that, or maybe she did, in which case she would know he was courting her. Well, now she knew for sure.

****

—Hi Doreen, Jim said holding a basket of laundry when she opened her door, cutting knife in hand.

—Oh, hi. What are you doing here?

—Could I wash my clothes ? The machines at my apartment house are on the fritz. Circuit problem or something. I've been on the road.

—How was Vermont?

—Made over fifteen hundred in three places. Got back last night.

—Make new contacts?

—Yeah. Things are coming together. I have to get over to the university for a workshop I'm hosting this afternoon, I'll meet the guests I'll be performing with tonight. So what are you up to? Working today?

—No. It's my day off. Just making a salad. Cleaned my first fish yesterday.

—What's the occasion?

—A client brought a salmon he caught off Seth Green Island. He's coming over tonight for dinner.

—You know, Doreen, you shouldn't eat fish from Lake Ontario.

—They say once a week is ok.

—I wouldn't do it.

—Ok, well thanks for the warning, she said as she rinsed the cutting board of stains from a ripe tomato. He stood in the hallway holding the basket until she looked up. Sure, you can do your clothes here.

—Doreen. I'm sorry about Hannah. It's not like we had sex.

—Well, you probably tried in the boat.

—No, I was probably feeling guilty for even being out there with her and it made me unsteady.

—Mm-hmm. What about all these changes with what you have to do to make a living? I'm just not sure who you are anymore. Or who we are. Or were.

—Would you give me another chance to show you?

—I'll think about it. She heard a perfunctory tone in her voice that she hadn't intended. I can do your clothes if you like.

—Thanks, Doreen. That's great. I'll be back later for them.

—Not too much later. My company will be here about six.

****

At the storytelling workshop Gloria Williamkee, whose father was full-blooded Cherokee, told her audience, —Explore your ethnic background. Research your genetic heritage. Every tradition has its own tales, German, Finnish or Japanese. But know the context. Don't tell somebody else's story just because you 'like' it. Respect borders. Especially in the case of Native Americans, be careful of taking what is not yours.

Jim thought, *Who are my people? The ones who said the hell with tradition? It's all been shaken up and watered down.* He had been planning on telling the Iroquois Creation story that night. *If I only tell stories from my own culture, what am I left with? Dick and Jane*?

He waited to go back to Doreen's till as close to six as he could, hoping to meet the fisherman. At 5:50 there was a hint of autumn in the cool evening air, smell of grilled salmon on the front porch, voices coming from the living room. When Doreen came to the door, there was an edge to her smile. —Sorry I'm late, he said.

—That's okay. My company came a little early. Henry, I'd like you to meet a friend. Henry Longar, Jim Fowler.

Jim stepped into the living room and shook hands with a tall smiling man who gushed with enthusiasm. —It's so good to meet you, he said. I understand you're a storyteller.

Jim nodded but before he could speak, Doreen said, —Yeah, he can't stay, he has a lot of stories to tell. She turned to Jim and held out the basket with his folded clothes. I cleaned out your pockets, she said in a rasping whisper. Jim saw the wrinkled paper on top of the clothes, flattened and smoothed, with a smiley face.

****

Jim opened the evening storytelling with "Spook Woods," a local variation on "King of the Cats."

Monday

(We spoke to the mother about the death of her son in the drive-by. We'll hear what she had to say, after this...)

As always Robert Haney was the first one in to work. It was his favorite time of day. His desk was clear, pens in a Harvard mug, post-it notes next to a bottle of hand sanitizer and an iris in a ball of blown glass all as he left them on Friday, The building was quiet, or would have been, if not for Frank, the night janitor finishing his shift, playing classic rock at top volume from the second floor while he mopped the hallway. Robert couldn't hear it from his office with the door closed but it bothered him to know that he could if he opened the door. He reminded himself, *if you want to go higher, don't mind the low places.*

The worst part of it were the deejays, even though their words were hardly more than a mutant echo on Frank's boombox in the cavernous hallways. They always had a man and a woman on the morning show in a pathetic attempt to generate a little sexual *frisson.* As if their witless banter about celebrities was anything but noise. Robert Haney knew if he simply walked down the corridor and let Frank see him, he wouldn't have to say anything. Frank would turn it down. But let him have his pleasure. God knows what little there could be in his life at that salary.

He turned on his computer and checked the latest reading test scores. How the high school compared with other schools in the district, and with other districts. Not that well, he saw. That was on Sue. She didn't ride the teachers. She let things slide. She called standards a dog and pony show. She didn't "believe" in testing, as if it mattered. She was the last of the old school liberal intellectual principals, and she was getting on. It might be time to retire her. That would require a little more finesse than he had used with the older teachers he had cleared out.

The phone rang. —Hello?

—Robert? This is Erin Brennan. I expected an answering machine.

—Good morning, Erin. I'm all about breaking expectations. And I bet I know what you've called about.

****

Jim Fowler was telling How Bear Lost His Tail to a group of kids surrounded by New York state landscapes from the Hudson River school. It was all because of Fox, he told them. They were from an after-school inner city recreation club on a field trip to the Memorial Art Gallery. They were all sitting on the floor, and four boys in a cluster felt on the verge of bubbling over so he stayed close to them,.

—Fox said like what you see? Pretty cool, huh? Sorry *you* don't have one like it.

These kids don't care where I come from, he thought. *They know a good story when they hear it.*

They sat sprawled or upright, among friends but in the story, their eyes on the teller.

Afterward, he went outside to the great white oak behind the gallery.

With all competing growth cleared away, it stood out unchecked, its branches spreading like gravity-defying rivers that flowed crystallized into the sea of sky, the green of its flickering upper leaves deepening before the coming bronze.

He used to pretend this tree was Yggdrasil, the mythical Scandinavian World Tree; or the Great Tree of Iroquois creation legend that the chief's pregnant wife dreamed had been uprooted, who had then said to her husband, *Make it so.*

But these days, he simply allowed this tree, growing on the grass by the parking lot, to fully enter his consciousness, which is to say, he did not have to pretend, but simply let it become the Great Tree.

****

—Mr. Haney, I've got the Board President for you.

—Put him on, Lee Ann.

—What's up, Robert?

—In a nutshell, Alan, this thing Friday needs our whole eye. I've already scored a new location, it's going to be in the auditorium instead of the boardroom. We're getting flyers out to parents. I want the *entire* board to be there and I want everyone on the same page.

—Teachers be there too?

—Maybe. But this is for the general public. We have a keynote speaker, Roy Kruzman, he'll talk about A.I. He's done TED talks, he's an engineer *and* a scientist. He'll get the crowd with us. I want to use him as a lever to get Board approval for a Special Bond Issue to bundle this whole STEM thing. Labs in the high school, A. I. projects, laptops for first graders, smartboards in every room, even the music and art rooms—

—Robert, I don't think the music and art teachers have their own rooms any more. They're all itinerant now.

—Whatever. But I want the Board to be there and on point because we're creating expectation, so it won't be out of the blue when we make the proposal in November. Are we clear? Oh, see if you can get some media love, will you?

After he rang off, Robert had an amusing idea. —Lee Ann? Would you send Sue a reminder to make sure we don't run out of bubble sheets for the field tests coming up next month?

Tuesday

(After an election commission declared he had lost by even more votes than had been previously counted, the former President told a rally in that state that the results showed the victory was his. We'll hear from several people at the rally about why they believed his claims, after this...)

When Jim Fowler entered the office of Director of Pupil Personnel, he noticed how Linda Crunch's eyes and nails and hair and clothes all interacted to both express her competence and to disrupt his breathing. —Let me get this straight, she said. You want to be a storyteller for the district?

—All levels, all grades. Teaching through narrative. Ballads, legends, history. Interdisciplinary. Creative thinking and writing.

Jim imagined he was sitting next to her, taking her in his arms. —Visual thinking. Metaphorical understanding. Cautionary tales. Social Studies through stories. Teaching meaning! Practical skills. Getting along, cooperative learning. I mean, Linda, wouldn't it be worth what I'm asking if you could cut down on violence *and* raise test scores?

He saw himself getting past her professional acumen, her carefully belted outfit loosening. He imagined her melting into his arms. He wanted this job.

—This is interesting. And boy, we have to do *something*. Jim waited while she quickly browsed the materials and silently checked and tallied her thoughts. There's a special events night coming up Friday. We have a speaker. I could float your idea to my boss and you could tell a story after the main talk. If you nail it, your plan might fly.

He left the office, feeling adrift. She wasn't who he thought she was. She was limited. Or was it he who was the limited one? He was Moses, pointing to the Promised Land, but it would be someone else who got there.

****

The world is inherently hierarchical, Robert Haney read in his office from Kruzman's book about the Singularity.

Of course, he thought, looking away, visualizing the old charts. Kingdom, Phylum, Class, Order, Family, Genus, Species. Forest, trees, branches, leaves, veins. Oceans, rivers, lakes. Creeks. Brooks. *Everything flowing one way.*

****

Jim felt it necessary to create a meeting with Doreen, since it didn't seem likely to happen on its own. He made a massage appointment.

—It's my back, mostly. Lower left, he said as he followed her up the stairs..

—Ok, two things, she said, turning around when they got to the top.

—I know, he said. Standard fee. And this is just a massage.

—Correct. She started to leave the room while he undressed.

—You don't have to worry about my privacy, he said.

—Just looking out for my own, thanks, she said as she descended the stairs.

Her attic was her massage room, redone in finished wood, dark colors and dimmed lighting, a cozy carpeted cavern with an A frame ceiling, Celtic harp music on an Echo.

He took off his clothes, put himself on the bench face down, pulled the blanket up to his waist and waited longer than it seemed strictly necessary. When Doreen came back, she poured a touch of rubbing oil in her palms and started working his shoulders. He tried to tell from her touch if she was still mad about the note, but what could he do if she was? After she palpitated each arm, she began to move down his back.

—You know, she said, I still don't get what happened. Do you?

—You mean with Hannah?

—No. With your job. He started to answer, but the face cradle was in his way. You were getting a good paycheck. Your broadcasting class voted you best voice. Didn't that mean anything?

—I already told you and anyway, what do you care? You kicked me out.

She pulled the blanket down slightly and made long, slow strokes down his spine. —Well, I'm glad you're doing something you like. You like it, right?

—Sure, he said, his speech constrained by the pressure on his jaws. It's what I was meant to do. Still seeing Henry?

—We're going roller skating tonight. He's asked me to chaperone a church group with him.

—I didn't know you skated.

—It's been a while. We'll see how long I stay upright.

—I'm sure he'll catch you if you fall.

She rested her hand gently at the base of his butt and make quick short pushes with her palm. —There's somebody else on the scene, since you're asking.

—Am I? Maybe I was just asking about my friend Henry.

—Right. He could hear in her voice that he had gotten her to smile. Well, I'm going to a movie with someone Wednesday, she said, now pounding him.

—What movie?

—That documentary about Snowden. Citizenfour.

He waited for the rest of it.

—I'm going with Robert Haney. I met him at school at fine arts night a few weeks ago, my niece had a picture in the show. He tried to hear if she was saying this because she wanted him to worry, or because she wanted him to know there was no hope, or because there *was* no hope. Turn over, she said, adjusting the blanket.

—Well, maybe I'll meet him. I might be performing at some kind of a school board presentation.

—Maybe I'll put in a good word for you if you're nice.

—I guess I'd rather you pretended we didn't know each other.

—Maybe we don't, she said, taking some more oil on her hands.

—Or maybe we could pretend we're new and start again, he said.

—You know, there are some things you just can't pretend.

He wanted to object, but got lost wondering if it were true.

****

A year ago spring, a friend had given Jim a tab of acid. Doreen was away visiting her mother in Elmira. He put on his shoes and swallowed the blue pill. He decided to take a walk through Highland Park,

It was one of the first warm nights and the air was translucent. He saw a girl, a young woman, sitting on a stone bench in a garden, waiting for someone. She was framed on both sides by forsythias and flowering redbuds. She waited expectantly, nothing nervous or preoccupied about her presence. He saw she was not simply another person, but an archetype of his imagination who was also a real woman. She was part of the stone bench, and she had been sitting there since the beginning of time.

As he entered the flow of the evening on the walk just above the budding lilacs, he saw that young couples holding hands were having intercourse. Everything was on a continuum.

He saw the sum of consciousness around him that pervaded it all was not strictly human. Things moved in a harmony that was not self-aware, because it was not a self. Light and shadow had substance. Down dark streets, cars projected streams of light. Sounds of horns joined the stream. He walked back toward the house in a mostly wordless play, a story with transitions. There was a Presence beyond his own in every scene. Since everyone he passed was a self, no one was; they were all unreliable narrators. Each person was a nesting doll with concentric identities. Whatever was generating all of this was right here.

Buildings quivered and collapsed, losing shape as he got sleepy. Going to bed, there were tears in his eyes at the thought of the orthodoxy of common wisdom, "All the lonely people," meaning, *All these separate selves.* But you could feel the continuous interconnected pulsing if you waited for it, which he knew the common wisdom could not do, nor could it cry or be in awe for a pulse so deep.

Everything was different the next morning. He saw the idea there was a reality apart from subjective experience was wrong, how the effort to bind everything into this single entity-- "reality"-- had the polis in a chokehold, even as the thing that actually bound it all was boundless. The school bus taking kids with their schedules of classes was no more or less structured or purposeful than a den of snakes. Each person was a whirlpool that flickered from moment to moment, a system of representations more complex than could be brought to words. The big world people think is *out there* is the same one that comes right up to you.

It was the next work day at the station he saw the strangeness of what *he* was doing. The elaborate ritual of the newscast, the predictable rising and falling of voice tones, the news, the stock markets, the weather filling psychic slots.

Hearing his own voice told him he was reading the news wrong, as if he were creating a solidifying perspective for listeners that would prevail. He began to rewrite stories in a way that expressed a presence and a connection to the audience. He linked stories, following one about a student shooting with one in which the state Board of Regents was requiring students to take more tests, —Which will again cut down on recess time in elementary school and take away such subjects as music and art from high school, he intoned. His boss explained this transition was heavy-handed, not to mention devious editorializing, and that he was putting too much feeling into what he was saying. It was then Jim realized he was in the wrong job. If there *was* a perspective that made any sense, it would not come from what he was presenting.

The problem was pretending he was not pretending, as if to pretend was something children did. Everyone around him was pretending to be serious, which made them sound pretentious.

Jim wanted to be serious about pretending. He wanted to seriously play.

****

—So, how do you like our kids, Doreen?

—They're very well-behaved, she said. But from the time she joined them in Henry's van, girls on one side, boys on the other, she felt their ditzy rectitude covering an empty space. She couldn't tell if the kids were repressed or blank. They were friendly, not personable. There wasn't anyone she wanted to talk to.

The arena was an open floor with bright neon cylinders on the periphery below dark geometrical shapes painted on the walls. The skaters were moving mostly counter-clockwise to a techno-dub soundtrack, multiple configurations of singles and families, couples and friends.

She had expected to skate with them, but when she understood that Henry saw their roles as guardians who did not actually participate, she joined him in the seats that fringed the rink.

—They're a good group of kids, he said. It's not easy being a teenager these days.

—Hey, was it ever?

—I guess I'm a little older than you, maybe, what? Six years? Seven? But when I was growing up we didn't have social media, what do you call it, Instagram, Twitter, texting, the rest.

—Maybe it's being a parent that's not easy, she said, as the teenagers' smiling faces floated past. I'm glad I'm not a parent now.

—But you want to have children, don't you?

—Some day, maybe. It's not a thing I think about much when I'm not in a relationship.

—I understand that.

—What about you? Do you want to have kids?

—Very much.

—Waiting for the right woman, huh?

Does she not know it's her, said a voice in one ear, while in the other: *does she really think I have options* —I believe, he said slowly, keeping an eye on the skaters, she is out there. Groups were breaking up and re-combining.

—It takes a leap of faith to link up with somebody, she said.

—But you've got to do it. I mean, don't you feel incomplete without that bond? Oh, there they go.

David, tall and exuberant, was holding hands with Natalie, who now had a radiant smile wherever she looked. —Well, they're good kids. Just got to keep an eye out.

—That's a good question, Henry, said Doreen. I'm not sure I would say *incomplete*. It's more a feeling of having potential. It's like I have a gift for someone, and I don't know who it's for, or even really what it is. I don't know if it's who I am or something I have to do.

He nodded as if in understanding, but thought to himself, *it's different for her. Maybe because she's younger. Or she doesn't need someone to share the burden.*

—One thing I don't need. A man who believes he has control over my body. Doesn't it say that somewhere in the Bible?

—Well, you know, he said equably, there's the *whole* quote, which sometimes goes unheard. 'The wife hath not power of her own body, but the husband; likewise, *also* the husband hath not the power of his own body, but *the wife*.' That's from Paul. He resisted the urge to cite chapter and verse.

—Hmm. So they have their hooks into each other. Doesn't sound too comfortable to me.

He tried to keep frustration out of his voice. —That's just the problem. Nobody's anchored down. Don't you see? If you're just living, if you're just floating, you haven't made it yours, you haven't planted your flag, a rogue wave can come out of nowhere and sweep you away. You have to secure what's given to you. You have tie those bowlines yourself.

They didn't speak for two revolutions of skaters, Doreen and Henry looking both at the kids and beyond them. —Maybe Buddha was right, she said. I never understood it before. Life *is* suffering.

—That's what the Crucifixion is all about, he said. And the Resurrection, he added.

Wednesday

(A new poll shows four out of five Americans...)

Jim went to Buffalo to tell stories at a small club. Before the performance he had dinner next door with his friend Carl who published books of poetry and fiction on his small press label, and a writer whose first book Carl had published, who had recently hit the big time with a book of short stories from Pantheon.

The visiting writer had a look of puzzled wariness when Jim told him what he did. —You tell stories you find in books? That's it? You don't write them yourself?

—Well, I give them life, said Jim. I give them presence... perspective.

—I'm not sure I know what to think of that, the author said.

—Well, come next door in a few minutes, you'll see.

Jim tentatively pecked at his salad, which was all he could eat before a performance, which this night occurred before a smallish, lackluster crowd which did not include Carl or the visiting writer, who went to a bar.

****

After they had ordered and the waiter brought their drinks, Robert proposed a toast. —Here's to dinner outdoors, he said. There won't be many more this year.

Doreen looked around as she raised her glass. —It's hard to believe it's October. A parking lot surrounded the restaurant; columns wound with vines and small white lights extended an arbor out to the street, with tables scattered around them on a lobe of grass. Next to it was a courtyard and garden in front of an old gothic-style cathedral.

—I love those old churches with blocks of rough stone and filials and towers and rose windows, she said.

Robert thumbed the stem of his wine glass. —We appreciate the old in the context of the new. Whereas when I look at you, I must tell you, I can't believe how good, how fresh you look this late in the day.

—Thank you. She put down her glass. You're very kind. You were good to get us seats here this late, after the movie.

—Did you like it?

—It has me thinking about surveillance being everywhere.

—Don't you think it's for our own good? We don't have anything to worry about if we're not breaking the law.

—But there's this unchecked power. Nobody even knows about it, except now they do a little, I guess. But nobody's regulating it.

—Why do they need to?

—Well, any time you have a secret agency monitoring ordinary people, which is itself unmonitored, —she looked for the thought— it's going to create criminals where there aren't any.

—How? The waiter had brought food, and Doreen found it useful to chew as she thought about what she thought, and how to say it. Finally, Robert said, You think law-abiding citizens will start breaking the law once they think they're being watched? That doesn't make sense.

—No, it's not like that...You know how sometimes you can't see something if you're not looking for it? What you see is what you're looking for. Things take on a certain arrangement.

—But it has to be there to see it. You aren't going to see it if it isn't there, unless you're hallucinating.

—So much is interpretation, she said. The world arranges itself according to our expectations.

—Which we are constantly revising. To keep up with things.

She swallowed some shrimp and took a sip of wine, looking past the vines to the cars on the lot. —When you're in a position of power and control, what's your motivation? You're not necessarily trying to keep up with adjustments. You're trying to *stop* things from adjusting.

—In a democracy—

—It's not a democracy! Nobody voted the NSA should be able to listen. Try some Jambalaya?

In the course of the evening, Doreen guided the subject away from surveillance, toward the value of storytelling in schools, to a man who appeared neither smitten nor besotted, but intrigued.

Thursday

(The Browns are favored by 6 ½ over the Lions, but can they cover the spread? We'll get the inside word after this...)

Sitting uncomfortably in Robert Haney's plush leather chair, Jim Fowler had not expected this meeting, but he understood Haney did not want Linda Crunch going over his head to the Board.

—So Linda tells me you want to tell stories to our students.

—I'd like to use storytelling to get their attention, Mr. Haney. Make them better listeners, better human beings.

—Well, we can talk about that. He spread his fingers across his meticulously appointed desk. What story were you proposing to tell tomorrow night? Robert Haney was thinking this could be good insurance if Kruzman turned out to be too dry.

Jim hadn't settled on a story but he saw it would be prudent to decide now. —I had a Japanese tale in mind, Jim said, keeping eye contact with Robert Haney. A carpenter is invited by the people of a village to build a bridge across a river. He promises to do it, but when he actually sees the river, he becomes full of doubt and fear. It's too big, too wide, too deep. Just then an ogre comes out of the river and builds a fantastic bridge from nothing. The carpenter wants to thank him with a gift. The ogre asks for one of the carpenter's eyeballs. Then he says he doesn't have to lose an eye if the carpenter can guess the ogre's name.

—Ah, said Robert. Like Rumplestiltskin.

—Yes, but the issue in this story is the use of the will in cognition. See, all his life he's been trained to think a certain way, that's how he became the best carpenter in Japan. But now he's called upon to think in a different way and he's lost.

—So what happens?

Jim often said, *Wait and see*, when someone asked this question, but Robert Haney didn't seem like the kind of man you said *wait and see* to. —Well, he gets so caught up in trying to *will* the name into his brain, he gets lost in a forest, and - I won't do this Friday, but this is actually a great story to do as a writing exercise in a classroom, where I stop at that point and say what happens next?

—So you have them try to predict the ending.

—Well, I don't actually ask them to predict. I just say, *give me an ending*. I make sure they understand there could be more than one. Their ending might be better than the book's.

—You know, the human brain's tendency to predict has always fascinated me, said Robert. Jim started to say, *this isn't trying to predict,* but held off. Research has shown we are constantly making hypotheses about what will happen next. Our brain is there to predict the future.

When Fowler looked blank, Haney went on. —Here, I'll show you. He turned around and went to his whiteboard. He wrote, WALK OVER TO THE ______. He stopped and looked at Jim. —What am I going to write next?

Jim said—Mmm. I don't know. File cabinet?

—Ah. Point is, your brain was already *buzzing* with possibilities. Everything in your cognitive processing software was bearing down on what that last word would be and trying to predict it. Maybe I'm getting too technical, I know you're a storyteller and you work with feelings. I'm just talking about what's behind the curtain, so to speak.

Jim interjected —Actually, when Bever and Chomsky found that decoding attention drops in reading at the ends of sentences, they hypothesized it was because readers were shifting focus from denotative to connotative, which involves subtle shifts in thinking, in other words, going from what is being said to what is meant. The reader slows slightly to summarize the information, because finding meaning is a more complex act of the brain than decoding, and the two actions constantly alternate with each other. Seeing Haney's quizzical look, Jim said, But you're right, people get in trouble when they think too much. Robert Haney never learned if the carpenter lost his eye.

****

Doreen put down her phone. She had a thought. She picked it up again and called her sister. —Henry has asked to me go with him to the School Board presentation.

—And?

—Should I?

—Why are you asking me?

—I just don't know if I want to go with him. But I'm not sure where that comes from.

—Do you like him? Has he asked you to church yet?

—No, but he probably will. He's okay. It's just being forced into making a decision, you know? Like am I leading him on if I just say yes?

—Well that's how it is when you're dating. It's harder to be casual. Things mean more than you intend them to. Maybe it's time to fish or cut bait, hah-hah.

—Hah-hah.

—Why don't you go, Doreen? He and Robert will be in the same room. It will give you some perspective.

—Yeah. I like that. Actually, Jim will be there too.

Friday night

(The world can be a dreary place, especially if you have indigestion...)

Jim Fowler tried to listen as Robert Haney introduced Roy Kruzman. It was always hard for him to listen to anybody when he was expected to speak afterward, because his mind kept going over how his own performance would play out.

But as Kruzman told of pattern recognizers and reducing complexity of data and nonbiological entities convincingly recreating emotional intelligence, Jim had a vision in which an intelligent mind became a disembodied eye, looking at itself as if from the outside. There was a thing separating it from itself and from everything else. That thing called itself Knowledge, and implied that it existed outside experience, -as if knowledge was not based on the collective experience of human thought - as if *this* Knowledge represented a thing superior to experience. As if the objective truth Kruzman spoke of was a thing experience was always trying to *get to*, but only this Knowledge *had* what experience couldn't attain. An experiential agent- i.e., a person- could only understand what consciousness was by abandoning her own experience and sucking on this straw of Knowledge provided by engineers and scientists like Kruzman.

Jim remembered a picture he had seen once, an artist's perspective of what our sun would look like from Pluto, never lighting up the sky as ours does but appearing as a contained glowing orb in the great blackness, like the star it is.

And he saw how the speaker, his urbane and affable manner frequently eliciting approving laughter with its gently self-effacing tone, was actually describing a terrifying abyss he did not recognize as such, because he had circumscribed everyone's senses, including his own, with an idea of knowledge of objective truth, so that all anyone really possessed was the cold holiness of spinning spheres. And he was leaning over the edge, confident in the strength of that protecting idea, not seeing it was only a thin wafer of abstraction, constructed of the flimsiest threads of his own entitlements.

All of it crystallized when Kruzman, working toward the subject of artificial intelligence, gave as example of nonhuman consciousness, a video of a giant squid under attack,—*or at least it thought it was,*-- and quoted an observer who thought it remarkable that a creature so different from humans could show what was obviously fear. —If we accept the observer's description and conclusion, Kruzman said, we must add giant squids to the list of conscious entities. But that would be an empathetic reaction, based on a self-centric or human-centric perspective.

Jim wanted to stand up and say *EMPATHETIC ISN'T SELF-CENTRIC! IT'S THE FUCKING OPPOSITE! EMPATHY MEANS SHARING THE MOMENT WITH ANOTHER! BUT YOU'RE NOT SHARING THAT MOMENT, YOU'RE TOO SECURE WITH YOUR PROBABILITIES AND YOUR GOALS AND YOUR GRANTS TO SEE REAL FEAR.*

But he didn't because he was going on next.

—So, in conclusion, you've heard it said there's a new world coming. But folks, I'm here to tell you it's not *coming* any more. It's here. Not only do we have the *ability* to create Artificial Intelligence, we've already done it, and you all have daily contact with it. Barcode scanning, Siri, Alexa, car sensors, GPS, Pandora, Google algorithms, these are just a few forms of non-biological intelligence which have become part of our daily lives. Questions?

There were a few children and teenagers scattered in the room. One boy near the front asked, —Mr. Kruzman, is it possible for machines to become conscious?

—Well- what's your name? Ben? Well, Ben, that's a very good question. What are the criteria you use for judging whether something is conscious or not?

—Um …Play chess?

—One of the things we do in science is break things down. Analytical thinking, Ok? So. Can it talk? Can it play games? Can it answer questions? Can it—

—Excuse me, said Jim, hand half-raised. You're not saying that talking is an indication of consciousness, are you?

—Well, that could be a way to recognize it.

—But we have things that make talking sounds that are not conscious. So we've actually eliminated that as a descriptor.

—Consciousness is a complex thing. We need multiple criteria in order to have a discussion. At any rate, the young man's question is one that a growing number of people are asking. That in itself indicates something. But if you look at the mathematical processes that are at work in artificial intelligence like Alexa, they look very similar to the evolution of the neocortex, which as we know, is responsible for the *Mona Lisa, Hamlet, The Ode to Joy*—

—Those works were achieved through inspiration, said Henry, from across the room.

—We can agree to disagree, the speaker said. It may be semantics.

—Didn't you ask us to engage in semantics by the questions you asked? asked Jim, still standing.

—Inspiration comes from God, said Henry, from across the room.

—Inspiration comes from breathing, which A.I. doesn't do, Jim said to Henry. Turning back to Kruzman he added, The neocortex didn't create the *Mona Lisa*. That was Leonardo da Vinci, the man.

Robert Haney said. —I think our time for questions is over. Let's give our speaker a well-deserved round of applause. He looked pointedly at Jim, who stood with folded hands amidst the clapping. Haney nodded and turned to the dais. —Dr. Kruzman, is there anything you would like to add as a final thought? Although this was technically a question, it ended with an emphatic drop, as if *a final thought* were the necessary and scripted antidote to the late digressions.

—Just this, said Kruzman, as if there had been no interruptions. We think our experience is marvelous. We don't realize that what is marvelous is our *brain*, the millions of neurons and pattern recognizers flickering at once. When we think we have an experience, what we are actually experiencing is our fragile sensory nerve fibers sampling the world around us, the light, the chemistry, the heat. That's all we know of the world. The rest of it is inferring through logic.

Jim sat down, saying so people around him could hear, —That's an autistic nightmare.

—Another round of applause, Robert Haney called out, after which he made a litany of announcements, some of which were repeated from earlier, concerning upcoming cross-country meets, tryouts for the spring musical, and details of the holiday schedule next month, before finally turning over the proceedings to the last item on the printed program, the storyteller.

Jim got up, looked over the audience till he saw Doreen, and said, —Don't shortchange experience. It's what brought you to the dance.

He told a story of how the best carpenter in Japan was asked by the people of a small village to build a bridge across a river, but when he got there found himself in over his head, so to speak. How a great ogre came out of the river and built a bridge so sublime it looked like a bridge to heaven. How the carpenter offered a gift in return, what would the ogre like? The ogre said, oh, he didn't really need anything, but maybe one of the carpenter's eyeballs would suit him fine. Just one!

Jim's audience heard the carpenter gasp, felt him cringe, shared in his terror and regret and shame. The bridge was there and he didn't want to be an ingrate, but he didn't want to lose an eyeball. And there was no question in the ogre's tone that he was ready to take it. In keeping with his generous spirit, the ogre told him he could keep his eyeball if he could tell the ogre what his name was.

Jim told the people how the carpenter stuttered, trying to think in the only way he knew; the ogre wanted him not to think, but to speak! A name, which he could say neither by thinking nor not thinking. But the carpenter didn't give up, and asked for another day. He walked into the mountain wilderness, tried to will the ogre's name into his brain, got lost and was ready to give up when he heard some children singing.

That is when, so Jim told the adults and the children and Henry and Robert Haney and Doreen and Linda Crunch and Roy Kruzman, and the entire Board of Education, (who Robert Haney was annoyed to see had stayed), the carpenter realized the singers were not ordinary children.

They were ogre children, and they were singing a song about the ogre, and they sang his name. The carpenter ran back to the village.

And *that* was how the carpenter ran down to the river next morning and the ogre rose up out of the churning waters and said —Do you know my name? and the carpenter threw out a few spoofs, at which the ogre laughed so hard the audience could feel it in their feet. But when the carpenter said the ogre's true name, the great being's mouth dropped open in disbelief and he howled in confounded rage HOW DID YOU KNOW? Jim Foley had to be careful not to spray the front row as the ogre plunged back into the water with a terrific SWOOSHHHHHHHHHHHHHH.

But everyone could see the bridge was still there, strong as a mountain, graceful as a willow.

People left satisfied and stimulated at the same time, even Jim, although he knew he could kiss that district storytelling job goodbye.

When Henry took Doreen home, he said, —It just amazes me how people can't see the forest for the trees. Where does he think this "amazing brain" came from but God?

—Thanks for the ride, Henry, Doreen said, and kissed him on the cheek. He started to ask her if she wanted to come to church with him Sunday night, but decided not to. He had the feeling she would say no.

Acknowledgments:

some of these poems appeared in the following books:

Ravine Street, White Pine press, 1977

Bold Cities and Golden Plains, FootHills, 2002

Walking Home from the Eastman House, self-published, 2011

September Rain

Finding the Way Home: Poems of Awakening and Transformation, White Pine Press, Buffalo, 2010

Bold Cities and Golden Plains, Ravine Street

Wedding at Black Creek Park	*Poetry Now*
Cloud	*Leaping Clear*
Diaspora	*The Aurorean*
Breathing Bright Air	*Country Journal*
The Day After I Came Back	*Tiptonville Poetry Journal*
Awakening on the Couch	*Lake Effect (Untitled)*
Decorum	*Visitant*
Guiniver	*BlazeVox*
The Teacher Who Told Stories	*Hyperterxt*

www.ingramcontent.com/pod-product-compliance
Lightning Source LLC
Chambersburg PA
CBHW050022170726
48282CB00025B/512
* 9 7 8 8 1 8 2 5 3 8 8 4 9 *